Five Traits of a Christ-Follower

five
traits of a Christ-follower

DOUG NUENKE
General Editor

NAVPRESS

A NavPress resource published in alliance
with Tyndale House Publishers, Inc.

NavPress is the publishing ministry of The Navigators, an international Christian organization and leader in personal spiritual development. NavPress is committed to helping people grow spiritually and enjoy lives of meaning and hope through personal and group resources that are biblically rooted, culturally relevant, and highly practical.

For more information, visit www.NavPress.com.

Five Traits of a Christ-Follower

Copyright © 2015 by The Navigators. All rights reserved.

A NavPress resource published in alliance with Tyndale House Publishers, Inc.

NAVPRESS and the NAVPRESS logo are registered trademarks of NavPress, The Navigators, Colorado Springs, CO. *TYNDALE* is a registered trademark of Tyndale House Publishers, Inc. Absence of ® in connection with marks of NavPress or other parties does not indicate an absence of registration of those marks.

Designed by Daniel Farrell
Cover photograph copyright © vetre/Dollar Photo Club. All rights reserved.
The Wheel® is a registered trademark of The Navigators in the United States. Used by permission of The Navigators. All rights reserved.

The Team:
Don Pape, Publisher
David Zimmerman, Development Editor

All Scripture quotations, unless otherwise indicated, are taken from the Holy Bible, *New International Version,*® *NIV,*® copyright © 1973, 1978, 1984, 2011 by Biblica, Inc.® Used by permission. All rights reserved worldwide. Scripture quotations marked ESV are taken from *The Holy Bible,* English Standard Version® (ESV®), copyright © 2001 by Crossway, a publishing ministry of Good News Publishers. Used by permission. All rights reserved. Scripture quotations marked NASB are taken from the New American Standard Bible,® copyright © 1960, 1962, 1963, 1968, 1971, 1972, 1973, 1975, 1977, 1995 by The Lockman Foundation. Used by permission. Scripture quotations marked MSG are taken from *The Message* by Eugene H. Peterson, copyright © 1993, 1994, 1995, 1996, 2000, 2001, 2002. Used by permission of NavPress Publishing Group. All rights reserved. Scripture quotations marked NLT are taken from the *Holy Bible,* New Living Translation, copyright © 1996, 2004, 2007, 2013 by Tyndale House Foundation. Used by permission of Tyndale House Publishers, Inc., Carol Stream, Illinois 60188. All rights reserved.

Some of the anecdotal illustrations in this book are true to life and are included with the permission of the persons involved. All other illustrations are composites of real situations, and any resemblance to people living or dead is coincidental.

Library of Congress Cataloging-in-Publication Data

  Five traits of a Christ-follower / Doug Nuenke, general editor.
    pages cm
    ISBN 978-1-63146-455-3 (parent) — ISBN 978-1-63146-539-0 (5 pack) 1. Christian life. I. Nuenke, Doug, date, editor.
  248.4—dc23   2015021856

Printed in the United States of America

21   20   19   18   17   16   15
 7   6   5   4   3   2   1

Contents

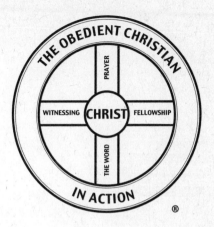

Foreword

DAWSON TROTMAN, who began The Navigators ministry among sailors in 1933, had a knack for developing illustrations to make spiritual truths easy to remember and apply. The most well-known of these illustrations is "the Wheel."

The hub of the Wheel represents Christ—the life and driving force of the Christian life—while the rim represents the lived environment of the obedient Christian, especially the people in the Christian's life. The two vertical spokes represent the Word of God and prayer, the principal means by which we draw upon the life and power of Christ. The two horizontal spokes represent fellowship among believers (what we now call "community") and witnessing (what we now call "evangelism"). Thus the vertical spokes emphasize our relationship with Christ, and the horizontal spokes represent our relationship with fellow believers and with unbelievers.

The Wheel may seem a bit simplistic to many today. In fact, I have at times been specifically asked to not refer to the illustration when teaching these principles to college students. But the basic truths of the Christian life illustrated by the Wheel are timeless. They are as old as the Word of God itself.

The five areas of Christian growth and competency covered in this devotional are a modern-day restatement of and enlargement on those fundamental principles illustrated in the Wheel. There is, however, one area of competency in the devotional that is not included in the Wheel: reproducing generations, an aspect of discipleship ministry that has been a primary emphasis of The Navigators from its early days. It was known as "the 2:2 principle," based on 2 Timothy 2:2: "And what you have heard from me in the presence of many witnesses entrust to faithful men who will be able to teach others also" (ESV). In fact, Dawson Trotman would often ask young men,

"Where's your man?" by which he meant, "Whom are you discipling for the next generation?"

Regardless of what strategies and techniques we develop in our discipleship, we must always keep going back to the basics. There is a famous story about Vince Lombardi, the legendary coach who led the Green Bay Packers to victory in several NFL championships and the first two Super Bowls. Once, standing before a team of disheartened players, he held out an oblong leather object and said, "Gentlemen, this is a football." Why would he say such a thing to a group of men who had played football from childhood and were now professional players? This was his way of saying, "We are going back to the basics of the game." This is what we believers need to do constantly. We need to keep going back to the basics of the Christian life. This book of devotional readings on the five primary areas of Christian growth is designed to take us all the way back to the fundamentals of Christian growth and competency. It is my prayer that this book will accomplish that objective in each of our lives.

Jerry Bridges
Author, *The Pursuit of Holiness*
Navigator staff member, 1955–2015

Introduction:

Getting Caught Up in the Love and Purposes of God

ARE YOU SOMEONE who is living with joy and purpose? Is the "song" of your life flowing freely from the person God has made you to be? Or do you, like many people, lack confident knowledge of God's love and purposes?

Do you believe that your life matters and that you are destined to bring healing to a broken world that needs what *you* bring?

The gospel is a redemptive ballad of God's love and purpose for a sin-drowned world. We are each destined to experience closeness with God and to draw others into that same relationship.

"To Know Christ and Make Him Known"—a phrase that has been the driving motivation for The

Navigators (and many other churches and mission organizations)—summarizes so much about a life dedicated to following Jesus. Jesus' appeal to some of His first disciples reflects a twofold calling: "Follow me, and I will make you fishers of men" (Matthew 4:19, ESV). They were called *to* Him and to work *with* Him.

To be a follower of Jesus means that no matter our career, our education, or our season of life, we are called to know Him and to work with Him in a spiritual harvest. This devotional is intended to help each of us walk closely with God and work more effectively with him in our world. You'll be led through five areas of growth for each of us.

1. *Walking with Jesus.* Howard Hendricks once said, "You cannot impart what you do not possess!" Jesus makes it clear that only as we are connected to Him will we experience a healthy spiritual life: "I am the vine; you are the branches. If you remain in me and I in you, you will bear much fruit; apart from me you can do nothing" (John 15:5).

2. *Knowing and living the Scriptures.* The Scriptures are God's means of bringing guidance and wise counsel to the life of each believer. The Holy Spirit guides us into knowing and living the truth of the Scriptures. As the psalmist said, "Your word is a lamp to my feet and a light to my path" (Psalm 119:105, ESV).

3. *Participating in community.* The life of discipleship is not meant to be experienced alone. God
   has designed us for community. We can only
   grow spiritually and be used by God as we are
   connected to others who love Him.
4. *Engaging with those who don't know Christ.* Every
   believer is called to engage with people in our
   broken world, where they live, work, study, and
   play. Each day opens opportunities for us to be
   salt and light among those who do not yet know
   Jesus and to bring hope found only in Him.
5. *Reproducing spiritual generations.* As we follow
   in the footsteps of Jesus, who invested in a small
   group of disciples, we aim to raise up others who
   will follow Christ and who themselves will help
   others as well. Psalm 145:4 assures us that "one
   generation shall commend your works to another,
   and shall declare your mighty acts" (ESV).

But before we immerse ourselves in these areas of
growth, there is something more foundational. Before
we do *anything*, our life in Christ is grounded in who
we are and who we are becoming in Christ Jesus. The
true test of life in Christ is our *character*: the extent
to which we are a reflection of the Spirit of God to a
watching world.

If the five traits discussed in this devotional are like
the five smooth stones that David grabbed out of the

stream to battle Goliath, our character is the sling. It is the *character of Christ* we envision being reproduced in the lives of everyday people (Philippians 2:1-8).

Your prayerful time in this book will help you connect with God's plan, conceived before the beginning of time. Growing in these traits will be a life-long process, and in each season of life, you'll find them adapting and shaping you into a partner with God in His kingdom mission. Your life will be used today but also will be creating a ripple of impact that will last for generations to come!

Dr. Doug Nuenke
US president, The Navigators

TRAIT ONE:

Walking with Jesus

Fruits of Living
in Connection with Jesus

JOE BROWN

*I am the vine; you are the branches. Those who
remain in me, and I in them, will produce much
fruit. For apart from me you can do nothing.*
JOHN 15:5, NLT

THERE'S A DIFFERENCE, in our world today, between
calling yourself a Christian and being connected to
Christ. As a young Christian I memorized John
14:21:

> Those who accept my commandments and
> obey them are the ones who love me. And
> because they love me, my Father will love
> them. And I will love them and reveal myself
> to each of them. (NLT)

At the time, I viewed this verse as a threat: If I really
love God, I reasoned, I'd better obey Him. Otherwise
He won't reveal Himself to me. He won't love me.

One day I was struck with an epiphany: This passage is not a threat; it's a promise!

One chapter after Jesus made this statement to
His disciples, He offered them an analogy: Jesus is

a vine; they (and we) are branches. The relationship between the two is organic. "If I love God," the logic goes, "I will obey Him, because He is filling me with new life and a new nature" (2 Corinthians 5:17). It's a done deal!

The life-giving power that flows out of Jesus, our Vine, flows into us, His branches. As we face the challenges and victories of life, we have Christ's strength, wisdom, and courage available to us "on demand." If we stay connected to Him, we can rely on Him to nourish and strengthen us by His love (obedience is not required for that love!). We even bear fruit. Only when we cut ourselves off from the Vine do obedience and fruit bearing become a struggle.

In John 14:23, Jesus reinforces the organic dynamic of our new nature: "All who love me will do what I say" (NLT). In Christ, the Father and the Son have moved into our hearts, taking up residence in our lives. Not only that, but the Father sends the Holy Spirit to teach and remind us of everything He has told us (verse 26). We may slip up in our obedience in the short term, but in the long run we can't help but obey because we have been possessed by the triune God; we draw our life direct from the Vine!

- Do you truly believe that God loves you regardless of what you do? Do you trust God enough to believe that you don't need to earn His love?

Spending Time with Jesus

MARTHA LAWRY

> *"Martha, Martha," the Lord answered, "you*
> *are worried and upset about many things,*
> *but few things are needed—or indeed only*
> *one. Mary has chosen what is better, and*
> *it will not be taken away from her."*
>
> LUKE 10:41-42

WE ALL LIKE TO HAVE our circumstances under control. How many times do we try to make things play out the way we want them to, or to assert our own will over seeking God?

This is demonstrated by Martha, who opened her home to Jesus, only to quickly busy herself with preparations for a meal. Meanwhile her sister, Mary, sat at the Lord's feet listening to what He had to say.

"Lord, don't you care that my sister has left me to do the work by myself? Tell her to help me!"

Martha wanted to put dinner on the table, regardless of whether the goal of her guest was to eat. The text tells us that she was "distracted by all the preparations." Her plea, "Lord, don't you care that my sister has left me to do the work by myself?" and her subsequent order, "Tell her to help me!" show that while she had made Jesus her guest, she was preoccupied with everything but Jesus.

Mary, by contrast, was focused on Jesus: She humbly sat, "listening to what he said." Mary and Martha and Jesus were all in the same place, but only Mary was with Jesus (see Luke 10:39-40).

When we try to grasp control of a situation, like Martha, we sacrifice our connection to God and His purposes. God's plans are superior to ours, and they include meaningful, consistent connections between us and Him. This connection is the "one thing" that is needed. Jesus wants us, like Mary, to spend time with Him and to seek Him and surrender to His superior plans.

- What is one situation you will likely face today that could distract you from your connection to God? How can you properly prioritize your time with God today?

- Where on your daily calendar could you intentionally book an appointment with Jesus? What time and place can you spend regular, uninterrupted time with Him?

Knowing and
Hearing from God

JOHN STARKE

*But when he, the Spirit of truth, comes, he
will guide you into all the truth. He will not
speak on his own; he will speak only what he
hears, and he will tell you what is yet to come.*

JOHN 16:13

A HEAVY GRAYNESS had settled over my life. It was
like daily walking through a cloud. This wasn't how
I pictured my life! I'd envisioned success, confidence,
and impact for God's kingdom, but getting out of the
dark became all I could think about.

Then one day, as I spent time praying and reading God's Word, His Spirit brought a question to
my mind. "If you never stop feeling like this, is
knowing and following Me enough for you? Am I
enough for you?" In other words, if I boiled away
all my "spiritual" and "reasonable" motives, was I
really just interested in feeling better? Or did I just
want Him?

The Spirit guided me into truth as I read Hosea
6:1-2:

> Come, let us return to the LORD;
>> for he has torn us, that he may heal us . . .
>> that we may live before him. (ESV)

Hosea calls Israel to openly acknowledge that their circumstances—fully orchestrated by *God*—are really painful. But he urges them to not stop there: Israel is to look beyond the scenery toward God's heart.

God unveils His intentions powerfully. He is willing to let us experience struggles and inconveniences as ways of knowing Him more deeply—"that we may live before him."

There are still days I live in the haze. But as I talk with God about what's going on and give Him the opportunity to speak truth back to me, He shows me that simply resolving my inconveniences is fool's gold compared to relating intimately with and following Him.

- Make a list of the hard things in your life right now. Tell God about them. Then, instead of focusing solely on "getting better," ask Him how He wants you to know Him better through them.

- Since growing a healthy relationship involves two-way communication, spend some time growing your relationship by talking to God as you would a friend and letting Him talk back to you through His Spirit and His Word. What is He saying to you through His Spirit of truth?

Becoming Like
Jesus in Our Attitude

MARK KIMMEL

*Have this attitude in yourselves which
was also in Christ Jesus.*
PHILIPPIANS 2:5, NASB

ATTITUDE IS LIKE THE WIND: It's something you can't see or touch, but you can see its impact.

We often go through life thinking little of how our attitudes shape our actions, our interactions with others, our very outlook on life. And even when we notice that our attitudes seem inappropriate, many times we don't know how to correct them.

The Scriptures show us that the journey of becoming like Jesus begins with our attitudes. The attitude of a follower of God, Paul shows us, was modeled by Christ,

> who, being in very nature God,
> > did not consider equality with God
> > > something to be used to his own
> > > advantage;
> rather, he made himself nothing
> > by taking the very nature of a servant.
> PHILIPPIANS 2:6-7

Developing an attitude of a humble servant goes against our human nature. But Jesus not only tells us that we are to become servants of one another; He also shows us that to be a servant is to be like Him! We can't pull this off ourselves. It is only as we live in close connection with Christ that His attitude and character will shine through.

Being aware of how our attitudes impact what we are doing, and then seeking the help of the Holy Spirit to change our attitudes, will help us overcome the pull of our humanness. As our attitude begins to resemble Christ's, we will find ourselves willing and acting in order to fulfill God's good purpose (Philippians 2:13).

- As you spend regular time with Christ, ask Him to reveal the areas of your character that need adjustment. Write them down and pray through them.

- How is your attitude impacting your behavior? Does it promote a servant's heart or a selfish heart?

- What is one thing you will commit to do to start to readjust your attitude to one that more reflects Jesus?

The Virtue of Love

GARY L. THOMAS

*Love the Lord your God with all your heart and
with all your soul and with all your mind
and with all your strength.*

MARK 12:30

CHRISTIANITY REQUIRES a tough fight. A heart that
is passionately engaged with God and His children is a
powerful weapon. Do you want to become holy? Then
open your heart and learn to feel deeply. Ask God for
the virtue of love.

How do we build a passionate relationship with
God?

1. *Ask God to help you.* If you have less attachment
   to God than you need to grow in holiness, stop
   right now and pray, "Lord, give me a love for
   You that is more powerful than any hunger for
   sin."
2. *Order your attachments.* Something that is not
   inherently sinful can still get in the way. On the
   other hand, sometimes love tells us to rest and
   "lighten up." Ordering your attachments is an
   art more than a science. It involves vigilance and
   discernment.

3. *Avoid competing attachments.* I can't consciously focus every minute on loving God. But I can keep a careful eye on the things I allow to draw my attention and my affections.
4. *Meditate on the loveliness of God.* There's a direct correlation between seeing Him with the eyes of faith, thinking about Him, and being bound by the cords of love.

Love has led individuals to abdicate thrones, relinquish inheritances, and move to foreign lands. Attachment to another person is truly a powerful experience. Attachment to God is an experience that changes us forever.

- Ask God today for a more passionate love for Him.

- What attachments are in the way of your passion for God? Ask God for discernment about how to rightly order your attachments.

- What do you love about God today? Keep a running list throughout the day as you watch for the loveliness of God.

Adapted from *The Glorious Pursuit*, copyright © 1988 by Gary Thomas. Used by permission of NavPress. All rights reserved. Represented by Tyndale House Publishers, Inc.

Sustained by God

KATIE HUBBARD

I lift up my eyes to the hills.
From where does my help come?
My help comes from the LORD,
who made heaven and earth.
PSALM 121:1-2, ESV

THE PHRASE "LOOK UP" flashes on the back of the city buses where I live. It is a catchy public awareness campaign, but for me it is much more. Every time I am stuck behind a bus, I see those words and I am reminded of Psalm 121.

In this life, we encounter suffering of almost unimaginable degrees. When walking the path of suffering, it is so hard to look up. I often feel like a hiker who has been so focused on the difficulty of the trail that she has completely missed the grandeur of the mountains that surround her. Yet when we look up, we see something very clearly. We see truth.

We do not walk alone. Our help comes from the Lord, who made heaven and earth. The creator God who "gives life to the dead and calls into being things that were not" (Romans 4:17) is our help.

Meditating on passages of Scripture like these

enables me to look up. I look up and I begin to see a different view. I see God. I see His help through His presence and character that never change. I see Him in the form of people who come alongside and help lift my load. Help is here; God is with us. We only need to look up, see, and believe.

- Whatever you are facing today, ask God to enable you to look up and see Him, His work, and His help.

- Do you have a story of where you've seen God help you or deliver you from a difficult situation? Thank Him for that help and let Him know that you still need Him each step of the way.

Knowing and Living the Scriptures

The Joy of Deep Nourishment

LINDY BLACK

Your words were found, and I ate them,
and your words became to me a joy
and the delight of my heart,
for I am called by your name,
O LORD, God of hosts.
JEREMIAH 15:16, ESV

I LOOKED AT THE FOOD in front of me. Everything looked and smelled delicious. The chef was guaranteeing satisfaction and pure delight! But until I filled my plate and ate, I had no idea the joy and fullness that could be *my experience*.

It can be the same with the Scriptures. I can know about passages. I may have heard someone talk about their experience in reading or studying. I can hear a verse quoted. But until I sit quietly with, read, reflect on, and am fed from the Scriptures, I am living on nothing but an imagined reality.

Jeremiah discovered the words of God and consumed them. He made God's words a part of himself. All good! But he goes on. The words *became* a joy and the delight of his heart.

Jeremiah ate—that was his part. Then he had an experience that surpassed his eating. Isn't that what we long for? Not simply *hearing about* the richness of the Scriptures. Not taking in *predigested food* from someone else. But knowing—deeply and experientially—nourishment, satisfaction, and joy in the words of God. It seems the more I taste, the more hungry I become.

- Ask God to give you an increased hunger for His Word.

- Consider how you can take time to be with God and be nourished from the Scriptures this week.

- Do you know someone who could be a guide of sorts for you as you begin to feast in the Scriptures? Put it on your "to do" list to call them and get time with them.

Instructions Fit for a King

STEVE RUGG

When he [the king] takes the throne
of his kingdom, he is to write for himself
on a scroll a copy of this law, taken from
that of the Levitical priests. It is to be
with him, and he is to read
it all the days of his life.
DEUTERONOMY 17:18-19

INTERACTING WITH SCRIPTURE is a wonderful thing, but to what end? Undoubtedly the kings of Israel, who wrote a copy of the law and read from it daily, knew God's words well. But what impact do these words have on our lives?

The second half of this passage highlights what can happen in our lives through this intimate knowledge of the Word of God:

He is to read it all the days of his life so that
he may learn to revere the LORD his God
and follow carefully all the words of this law
and these decrees and not consider himself
better than his fellow Israelites and turn
from the law to the right or to the left.
DEUTERONOMY 17:19-20

Through our time in the Scriptures we first gain *a reverence and awe* for the Lord, the God of the entire universe. We see a clearer picture of who He is and what He has done.

We are also more likely to *obey God's words* as we interact with them; while knowing God's words is not a guarantee that we will follow them, *not* knowing them *is* a guarantee that we *won't*.

It is the third outcome from spending time in God's Word, however, that is most intriguing to me. What is it about reading and studying Scripture that *builds humility*? I believe one reason is that we get a more accurate view of how much greater the Lord is than we are. Another reason is that the Bible shows us numerous examples of people choosing paths that are contrary to God's desires. If so many of them disobeyed, certainly we are susceptible as well. May we be people who take our cues from Scripture as we obey the Lord and demonstrate humility—before Him and the people around us.

- What are the hurdles you experience in having regular time with the Word of God?

- Do you notice a humility that comes from your interaction with Scripture? Why or why not?

- What can you do to ensure that your times in the Bible lead to specific actions and applications?

I Need to Know God's Path!

TOM YEAKLEY

Your word is a lamp for my feet,
a light on my path.
PSALM 119:105

"LORD, I WANT TO KNOW your will for me in this. Please show me what I should do. I've got a lot of good-looking options in front of me and I'm confused on which one to pick." How often have we expressed these sentiments or something similar?

We often think of knowing God's plans as a search for the proverbial micro-dot in the universe. But really it is like following a broad expressway that leads us into our God-ordained personal destiny. He does not want us confused or uncertain about the path we are to follow, and He gives us guidance from the Bible that we may continue to follow Him.

As we interact with the Scriptures, we can use the following questions as means for direction in our particular circumstance:

1. Is there a command to obey?
2. Is there a principle to apply?

3. Is there a promise to plead?
4. Is there an example to imitate?

For many of us, the challenge is not in knowing the will of God; rather, it is doing the will of God that stretches us! When God speaks we must obey His commands, apply His principles, and imitate His examples. But we may also plead for Him to fulfill His promises. When we engage the Scriptures with these four questions, we hear from God and, by faith, we can walk into an unknown future with confidence.

- Are there places in the Scriptures where God has been speaking to you? What passages stand out in your thoughts? Meditate on these passages, asking God to clearly guide you.

- For you, is it more difficult to discover God's desires or to obey them?

- Is there something that God has been saying to you from the Scriptures that you know you need to apply and obey? Consider writing it down and putting it into action.

The Countercultural
Word of God

PATRIECE JOHNSON

Sanctify them by the truth; your word is truth.
JOHN 17:17

ONE EASTER, while the children were hunting in the backyard for plastic, jellybean-filled eggs, the adults noticed that the children were intentionally leaving some eggs behind, thinking they were empty. When the hunt was over, the kids were surprised to learn that these eggs were not empty but were filled with dollar bills. Despite their lack of popularity, these eggs were special, set apart, and carried great value.

Just as with the eggs left behind, I have had to learn that a "sanctified" life—a life set apart as different by living out the truth found in God's Word—may not be highly regarded in the world, but it is of infinite value. Living the Word of Truth means that my words, attitudes, and behavior will likely be misunderstood by, in conflict with, and even offensive to the patterns of this world. But believing God's Word enough to obey it will draw some people to the hope and light of Christ and will help us be more like Him.

As followers of Christ, how do we embrace the

sobering reality that the world might reject us? First, we fight against taking *rejection* personally. People are not rejecting us but the Lord, to whom we all will give an account (John 12:48). Second, we understand that we are living for an eternal kingdom and seeking an eternal *reward* instead of living for the acceptance and approval of man (Galatians 1:10). Lastly, the Word of God is constantly looking for soft, fertile hearts to penetrate, producing eternal fruit. God transforms us through the Word; our increasingly obedient lives will often woo people to God and will have *restorative* value to both ourselves and others (John 17:17-18).

Just like the Easter eggs that were passed up, believers who follow God's Word in obedience will inevitably be misunderstood. May we see both the greater value of allowing the Word to set us apart for Christ's eternal purposes in our lives and the many who *will* be ready to seek after Him.

- What characterizes someone who has been set apart by the Word of Truth?

- How has your obedience to the Word of God led to rejection?

- How has your obedience to the Word of God led to restoration?

The Bigger Picture Behind Small Verses

LEONARD SWEET

> *"A man named Nicodemus . . . came to Jesus at*
> *night. . . . 'How can this be?' Nicodemus asked."*
> JOHN 3 : 1 - 2 , 9

CAN YOU RECITE FROM MEMORY the most famous Bible verse, John 3:16, "the gospel in a nutshell"? I bet you can:

> For God so loved the world that he gave his
> one and only Son, that whoever believes in
> him shall not perish but have eternal life.

Now recite John 3:15. No? John 3:14? How about John 3:17?

It wasn't until well into my ministry that I realized that while I had memorized hundreds of Bible verses, I had never memorized a Bible story. I had "hidden . . . in my heart" (Psalm 119:11) only the parts, not the whole.

The Bible is too often stripped of story and mined for minutiae; it becomes not "the greatest story ever told" but the greatest story *never* told, or *half*-told.

Nicodemus—Jesus' conversation partner in John

3:16—is the patron saint of all of us suffering from "versitis." He could understand truth as text, as words, as laws, as left-brain logic. But Nicodemus could not process Jesus' right-brained imagery and poetry of being "born again" (John 3:3). A faith that doesn't know what a metaphor is can't sustain us, nor can it grasp who God is and how God relates to us. Meaning in life is not found from reducing things into smaller categories and making finer distinctions. Meaning in life is found in putting things together, connecting the dots, and getting the "big picture." To testify to truth is not to versify but to storify.

- Think of some verses you've committed to memory. Open the Scriptures and read each verse in context. How is your understanding of the verse changed?

- Is there a person in your life this week that could benefit from hearing an important concept about Jesus or a story from the Scriptures that gives hope? Who is that person and what could you share?

Adapted from *From Tablet to Table*, copyright © 2014 by Leonard Sweet. Used by permission of NavPress. All rights reserved. Represented by Tyndale House Publishers, Inc.

Let the Scriptures Lead You

JOE MASCHHOFF

*You study the Scriptures diligently because
you think that in them you have eternal
life. These are the very Scriptures
that testify about me, yet you refuse
to come to me to have life.*

JOHN 5:39-40

WHEN JESUS CHALLENGED the diligent study of
Scriptures in John 5, he was addressing religious leaders who knew the Scriptures very well. They likely
knew all sorts of answers, facts, details, examples, and
themes. And yet Jesus chastised them publicly, appar-
ently without hesitation.

They were missing something fundamental.

Our hearts are gripped with the desire to live out of
the Scriptures—to know them and to lead from them.
In order to fully grasp what this means, however, it
might be helpful to consider what it does *not* mean. Our
zeal for living out of the Scriptures is not for the sake of
knowing more or for impressing our friends. Our pride
can push us toward finding life in knowledge—even
knowledge of the Scriptures! However, what we are
after—what we must be after—is God Himself.

When we lose sight of the pursuit of God in our study of the Scriptures, we miss something fundamental. Living and leading from the Scriptures does not primarily give us more Bible knowledge; when properly framed in the pursuit of God, it distinguishes us as sons and daughters of the Most High God.

The Scriptures can be a doorway to God. They can direct us toward knowing, experiencing, trusting, and loving Him. When we lead from the Scriptures, in actuality we are letting them lead us to Him.

- Study a passage of the Scriptures. How does this passage help you know God more deeply?

- How does this passage help you live more fully into your identity as a son or daughter of the Most High God?

TRAIT THREE:

*Participating in
Community*

The Call to Community

ROBERT DANIELS

*Day by day, attending the temple together and breaking
bread in their homes, they received their food with
glad and generous hearts, praising God
and having favor with all the people.*

ACTS 2:46-47, ESV

THE EARLY CHURCH was defined by four devoted
actions:

- the apostles' teaching
- fellowship
- breaking of bread
- prayer

These four devoted actions happened in response to
the gospel taking root in the hearts of those who came
to faith in Jesus Christ, and in the community that
emerged in the midst of them.

The idea of community rings loud in Acts 2. They
were loyal in their fellowship with one another. Wor-
ship happened in community. Needs were met in
community. Evangelism happened in community. The
presence of the Lord dwelt among the people in community.

Community today looks very different. We are content with a Sunday service, a coffee shop meeting, and a Bible study every now and again. But should we be? If we say we love Jesus, we will also personally and authentically engage in love in an expression of his bride, the church. Love is action, and action propels us toward one another. A right response to the gospel of Jesus Christ is to engage in community.

The early church lived selflessly around each other, for each other, as a community of believers. "And the Lord," we are told, "added to their number day by day those who were being saved" (Acts 2:47, ESV).

- What does your community look like? Are you engaged and active in a way that lets people know what your needs are, and vice versa?

- Are you devoted to a particular group of Christ-followers? Is your group connected naturally with those who don't yet know Jesus? How does your love for each other help others know that you are Christ's disciples (John 13:35)?

A Humility That
Results in Oneness

*Make friends with nobodies; don't be the
great somebody.*
ROMANS 12:16, MSG

TRUE COMMUNITY AND FELLOWSHIP are often missing across the Christian landscape. This is in stark
contrast to what Jesus prayed as His "goal" for His
followers:

> For all of them to become one heart and
>   mind . . .
> So they might be one heart and mind
>   with us. . . .
> Then they'll be mature in this oneness,
> And give the godless world evidence
> That you've sent me and loved them.
> JOHN 17:21-23, MSG

To achieve this oneness, we must recognize that
each person has something to offer, something to
share, something we can learn from. We need to get
over ourselves! We need to exercise humility. If we're
humble, we'll never look down on anyone. Despite our

weaknesses and shortcomings, we determine to look up to them and see them as God wants us to see them.

In Romans 12, Paul echoes Jesus' prayer for a unity of the faith and a common mindset. Paul is not suggesting, of course, that we all must think exactly the same thing about every issue. Instead, he calls on us to "be good friends who love deeply" (verse 10, MSG). We are to demonstrate the love, unity, and sacrifice that can only be found through our personal relationship with Christ.

We will grow and engage in "true" community with one another when we take joy in being humble, seeing each person as valuable, becoming more transparent, and blessing one another without judgment. True community comes from this kind of practical oneness, and by this oneness the world is shown Christ.

- In what areas of your daily life do you need to be more humble, loving others more than you love yourself?

- Is there someone in your life that, despite differences, you can demonstrate love, unity, and sacrifice to encourage them in Christ?

- When was the last time you recognized that God might be speaking through someone you thought you had nothing to learn from?

Running Alongside

FELIX COLONNIEVES

*Therefore, since we are surrounded by such a great
cloud of witnesses, . . . let us run with perseverance
the race marked out for us.*
HEBREWS 12:1

ONE OF MY FRIENDS ran the Leadville 100 last August.
That's a legendary "race across the sky": one hundred
miles at an elevation averaging ten thousand feet above
sea level, complete with a mountain pass and a river
crossing. He did really well by himself for the first fifty
miles, but there was great relief when his pacers joined
him, carrying his water, gels, and food for the last fifty
miles. They kept him on a pace to finish well, and they
helped to motivate him toward the end as the race
become more mentally than physically challenging.

I was one of my friend's pacers. There were times
when he was happy to have me run behind him, just
knowing I was there to keep him on pace. Other
times—in the middle of the night, or after twenty-three
hours of nonstop action—I would tell him a story or a
joke to keep his mind engaged. Then there were times
when he just wanted us to let him "be," so he could "get
in the zone." These were the most difficult parts for me
personally, a natural extrovert!

Pacing is a good analogy for how we relate to one another in the life of faith. We aim to help one another reach maturity in our lives and relationships with Jesus Christ—what Paul calls the "finish line" (1 Corinthians 9:26, MSG). We come alongside one another, providing guidance and food through counsel in the Word of God, simply sharing a story, or even just accompanying one another through stressful times. Sometimes our friends just want us to offer a shoulder to cry on; sometimes they simply need to be left to "get in the zone" at their own pace.

With the help of his crew and his pacers, my friend reached the Leadville 100 finish line. It is my hope that we will not neglect the discipline of teaming together to help one another reach our own finish line as a community of faith.

- Who are the people you are "running" with in your life in Christ, "pacing" one another in walking with God and in your ministry to others?

- Do you find it hard to let your friends "get in the zone" at their own pace? How can you support them without imposing your pace on them?

- Who is someone who needs your help this week to come alongside and encourage them in their life and walk with God?

Words That Give
Courage to Faith

JEAN FLEMING

*But Caleb quieted the people before Moses
and said, "Let us go up at once and occupy
it, for we are well able to overcome it."*
NUMBERS 13:30, ESV

THE SPIES RETURN from scouting out the Promised
Land. All twelve spies agree that the land is good, very
good. But ten spies terrify the people with a scary
assessment: The people are strong, the cities are big,
and there are giants in the land.

I imagine everyone talking at once, that nervous,
high-pitched, unsettling babble inspired by fear. This
is a murmuring that looks for someone to blame
(Numbers 14:2). Complaining infects and under-
mines. It impedes progress. The negative outlook of
these ten spies leads the people to prefer the unre-
deemed stability of slavery over following God by
faith into the Promised Land. This is the grumbling
that God hates.

Into this atmosphere Caleb and Joshua speak
(Numbers 14:6-9). They turn the direction of the conversation from fear to faith, from mob murmuring to

united action, from focus on the obstacles to reliance on the presence and promises of God. They attempt to speak words that would give the people courage to trust God and do what He called them to do. While Caleb and Joshua's words didn't change the mind of their generation, those words did lay the foundation for the next generation's entry into the land. For when murmuring ceased and faith emerged, the people of God moved from capitulation to stouthearted obedience.

- Are you more inclined to murmur out of fear, or to act on faith? Ask God to make you increasingly less like the ten spies and more like Caleb and Joshua.

- Is anyone in your life currently murmuring? How can you help to quiet their fear and strengthen their faith?

- Is there a present issue in your life that poses a large challenge where, like Caleb and Joshua, you need to move from murmuring to responding in faith and giving courage to others involved?

Suffering and Rejoicing Together

RACHEL JONES

*If one part suffers, every part suffers
with it; if one part is honored,
every part rejoices with it.*
1 CORINTHIANS 12:26

WE ARE THE BODY of Christ. Whether or not we see eye to eye or naturally enjoy one another's company, the fact remains that in Christ, believers are one unit.

We are invited, as members of the one body of Christ, to rejoice together. Sometimes this is hard. Comparison, pride, envy, and bitterness are divisive sins that destroy community. But rejoicing isn't fancy or complicated. Laugh together, congratulate someone, throw a party: God is glorified in our friend's honor, and that is reason to rejoice. Jesus Himself went to a friend's wedding party (see John 2)!

As the body of Christ, we are also invited to suffer together. This is community, but it is also ministry: When we commit to entering into one another's suffering, we bring, through the Spirit, the comfort of the God of all comfort. Suffering together isn't fancy or complicated either. Sit in silence with someone who grieves. Send a note or carry a meal to those facing deep disappointment. Express, with or without words, that you walk together through the valley of the shadow of death. Christ gave an example by traveling to be present with his mourning friends and cry with them (John 11:17-37).

When the body of Christ suffers and rejoices together, there is scant opportunity for sin to creep in and steal, kill, or destroy. When we enter into the emotional realms of rejoicing and suffering with a handful of friends, we embody the kind of community that God intends for His people.

- Is it easy or difficult for you to engage with others in the emotional realms of rejoicing or suffering? Which one takes more effort for you?

- Name one or two brothers or sisters who are going through a period of suffering or are rejoicing because of evidence of God's goodness.

- What can you do this week to suffer or rejoice with them? Write it in your to-do list or put it in your schedule.

The Healing
Effect of Confession

MATT LETOURNEAU

*Therefore, confess your sins to one another and pray
for one another, that you may be healed. The prayer of
a righteous person has great power as it is working.*
JAMES 5:16, ESV

TO ENGAGE IN TRUE COMMUNITY, one must be
willing to take relational risks. Sadly, many people
are unwilling to take risks—partly because they at
one time drummed up the courage to share real life
struggles, only to be hurt as a result. They may continue to do their Christian duty, show up at their
community groups, and go through the motions
of "surfacey" Christian community. "Transparent
enough," a friend of mine says cynically, "not to look
suspicious." Broken confidentiality, a lack of empa-
thy, or other such hurtful responses can lead to the
thought that nobody on this side of eternity under-
stands us or can really walk with us in life. However,
this is a debilitating lie and is not God's desire for us!

James's call to "confess your sins to one another
and pray for one another" points to prayer and confession as powerful community-building practices.

In fact, the context reinforces that soul-level prayer is a primary restorative activity, provided for every believer. The kind of prayer James refers to is in response to open-hearted confession of sin. That's a risk, but one that opens us up to the care and influence of those to whom we bring our vulnerabilities and shortcomings. When we confess our sin and vulnerabilities to trusted friends, we become people who experience healing—healing that God provides for us through true community.

- Are you a person who has learned to be "transparent enough to not look suspicious"? Or are you openly confessing your sin to mature believers in a trusted community?

- Do you believe God when He says that there is healing in the confession of sin to your trusted friends? How does confessing to others bring healing?

- Is there something on your mind that you need to confess to a trusted friend, pray about with them, and begin the process of healing?

TRAIT FOUR:

Engaging with Those Who Don't Know Christ

Jump into
the Neighborhood

ALAN ANDREWS

*The Word became flesh and blood,
and moved into the neighborhood.*
JOHN 1:14, MSG

WHEN MY WIFE AND I first moved into our very multi-cultural, poor Phoenix neighborhood, we wondered how we would integrate into our new community. I will never forget Kit Danley, founding director of Neighborhood Ministries, telling my wife Becky and me to "jump into the community; the water is fine!"

Some of our new friends, we discovered, were already in the kingdom of God; others were on their way, while many others were (and still are) far from Jesus. But five years later the thing I find most comforting is that we are part of the fabric of the community. Every day we get up with the intention of being the loving presence of Jesus right where we live, work, and play.

Sometimes that presence involves just helping others with living life; on other occasions it involves a Bible study or a teaching time. Much of our time is given to leading enterprises that help engage the community in sustainable businesses. I have found, however, that moving into the neighborhood is more about friendship than anything else.

So often I find many of my friends and acquaintances talking as if they have to go somewhere—a foreign mission field or something like that—to live and minister among people who have yet to know Christ. Jesus' life is a stark contrast to this way of thinking. Jesus was not afraid to get into the soil and mud of the community He served. He became part of the very fabric of His hometown and home region. It seems to me that we all must learn to "jump in" to our neighborhoods, our workplaces, and other communities we may be part of. When we do, we find that the water is fine after all, and our ministry is more neighborly, more natural—more loving and present.

- What intimidates you about representing Jesus to your neighbors, friends, and coworkers?

- What are one or two specific ways you can purposefully be more of a loving presence in your community?

Reflecting the Light

DARRELL AND CINDY JOLLEY

*So all of us who have had that veil removed
can see and reflect the glory of the Lord.
And the Lord—who is the Spirit—makes
us more and more like him as we are
changed into his glorious image.*
2 CORINTHIANS 3:18, NLT

HAVE YOU EVER BEEN ENTERTAINED by a beam of light? Maybe one reflecting off a mirror or the face of your watch? In the right place, holding the right position, you can direct the light into whatever shadows you like.

The moon is like a mirror or a watch. It does not generate its own light; it simply reflects the light of the sun toward the darkness of the earth.

Like the moon, we who have had the veil removed in Christ reflect the light of the Son into the spiritual darkness of those around us.

Two things are necessary to reflect light into a dark place. First, we must be *in the light*. It is the work of God's Spirit to transform us into His likeness with increasing glory. It is not our work. If we walk in the light of God's presence, we will reflect His glory automatically, just as the moon cannot help but shine with the light of the sun.

Second, we must be *intentionally positioned* to shine. If our light doesn't shine into darkness, what good is it? We put ourselves in positions where we focus the light of the gospel into the lives of those around us who are walking in darkness.

Light is fascinating. So is God. And we, with unveiled faces, have the privilege of conveying our fascinating God to those who need His light and life.

- Are you walking in the light of God's presence, allowing Him to transform you into His likeness? How can you do so more purposefully?

- Who are the people already in your life to whom you can reflect the light of the gospel? What activities can you join them in to build the relationship? What questions can you ask to open doors for reflecting light into their lives?

Loving and Being
among Broken People

JANE KIRKPATRICK

Who needs a doctor: the healthy or the sick?
Go figure out what this Scripture means:
"I'm after mercy, not religion." I'm here to
invite outsiders, not coddle insiders.
MATTHEW 9:12-13, MSG

JESUS, AS SWISS THEOLOGIAN Jean Le Clerc observed, "ate good food with bad people." This habit often got Him into trouble, like the time Jesus was eating supper at Matthew's house, when "a lot of disreputable characters came and joined them." The Pharisees saw this happening and took offense. "They had a fit," we are told, "and lit into Jesus' followers. 'What kind of example is this from your Teacher, acting cozy with crooks and riffraff?'" (Matthew 9:10-11, MSG).

It intrigues me that the Pharisees "lit into Jesus' followers" when Jesus Himself was right there in front of them. Perhaps they recognized the power of Jesus and feared facing it directly. Nevertheless, this topic was central to His ministry on earth, so He did respond to them. He urged them to turn to Scripture to understand His behavior: Was He consorting with riffraff, as they feared, or was He bringing healing to outcasts and broken people?

Sometimes people observe our commitment to service in the name of Christ and question our motives: Why risk our reputation? Why waste our talents on people who don't enhance our brand? Why not use our education or life lessons for more personal gain? In a world where getting ahead and making a name is the message of the times, they see us as misguided. We can be tempted to agree with them.

When we doubt our purpose in a world where people seem to be rewarded for chasing false gods—when we falter or put on our own Pharisee hats—Jesus tells us to turn to Scripture. He reminds us of our mission: that we are doctors bringing healing to the sick right where we are in our daily lives. Daily we can rediscover that the lesson of His healing life—and our own—is not religion; it's mercy. It's love. Who are the broken, the sick, the "riffraff" God is calling us to today?

- What Scriptures do you turn to for your own healing and as a reminder of our mission of mercy and love?

- Are there any "riffraff" with whom you need to develop a closer relationship for the sake of the healing gospel? Who are they? How can you engage them this next week?

Motivated by
and Sharing Love

AL ENGLER

*"Love the Lord your God with all your heart and
with all your soul and with all your mind." This
is the first and greatest commandment. And the
second is like it: "Love your neighbor as yourself."*
MATTHEW 22:37-39

MY WIFE, IRIS, and I live in a twelve-unit townhouse
complex in the middle of Seattle. Our neighbors
include Buddhists, homosexual partners, hetero-
sexuals living together outside of marriage, and vocal
atheists. We know them by name and genuinely enjoy
them. They are software designers, joggers, skate-
boarders, feminists, liberals, secular, and all-around
interesting and fun people. Since moving in, we have
had them over for dinner, taken care of their pets,
shared meals in their homes, attended parties with
them, weeded their flowerbeds, cut their grass, orga-
nized a neighborhood watch with them, and given
them Christmas cookies.

Iris and I love God. We both are deeply in touch
with the miracle of how God reached down and
changed the course of our lives. We live in freedom,

joy, and peace because of Him. We know that, apart from a relationship with God through Christ, our lives would be empty and meaningless. We love Him because He first loved us.

That love of God compels us to love our neighbors, as Paul said it would: "Christ's love compels us, because we are convinced that one died for all, and therefore all died" (2 Corinthians 5:14). We long for our neighbors to know Jesus. We desire to see the life of Christ reproduced in them, and we trust that, as we obey the greatest commandment (love God) and second-greatest commandment (love your neighbor) in their midst, God is at work.

- How does God's love for you motivate you to love others?

- What is the relationship between love and the gospel?

- Who are some people close to you whom you love with God's love? What are some practical ways you could love them?

Engaging with
People Different from Us

ABU MANNAR

Now he had to go through Samaria.
JOHN 4:4

IF YOU WANT TO WALK with God, you won't always
wind up where you expected.

If you want to go to Galilee, you don't go through
Samaria. Jesus wanted to go to Galilee. And yet He
went through Samaria. Why? Because He "had to."

When Jesus went to Samaria, He was going out
of His way. Jews did not try to find ways to hang
around Samaritans—they had history and were not
on friendly terms. Yet Jesus kept going. He went out
of His way to talk to a Samaritan woman there. He
was fully aware that He was stepping over not one
but two barriers: the social barrier between Jews and
Samaritans, and the cultural barrier between men and
women. By all rights, this conversation should not
have happened. And yet it did.

When Jesus and the Samaritan woman were done
talking, she ran to tell her story to her people, complete
with an invitation: "Come, see a man who told me
everything I ever did" (John 4:29). They soon urged

Jesus (a Jew, with whom Samaritans did not associate) to stay with them. So He delayed His trip to Galilee again and stayed among them for two full days. He stayed to engage with people who didn't know Him yet, even though they were different from Him.

How hard it must have been for the disciples. They wanted to go to Galilee, and now here they were, stuck with the Samaritans, of all people. But sometimes that's what happens: Walking with God will take us to places we don't expect, with people we may not be familiar with; and there we'll see God do a great work.

- With whom can you identify in this story? The Samaritan woman? The disciples? Jesus? In what ways are you like each?

- Where is your Samaria—that place where you're glad you never have to go? How might God use you if you went there?

- Are you engaging with people different from you? What have you learned and seen God do through the experience?

Whatever It Takes

JEN HATMAKER

I have become all things to all people so that by all possible means I might save some. I do all this for the sake of the gospel, that I may share in its blessings.
1 CORINTHIANS 9:22-23

IF WE'RE GOING to win people to know Christ, then let's win people. We do whatever it takes—within the boundaries of law and neutral practices without moral significance—to attract people to the glorious mercy of Jesus.

If people are offended by God Himself—by His authority, His Word, His Son, His history—they will ultimately have to wrestle with Him. But if they are offended by our representation of God, then we'll answer for our arrogance. We can help that, and we had better do it.

Jesus ate with sinners, created wine for partygoers, fished with fishermen, held the children of mothers, taught in the temple with teachers, and worshiped in synagogues with the faithful. All things to all people, not bound by convention, public opinion, appearance, legalism, or even His own rights.

Not everyone we touch turns to gold, or to Jesus.

They are not all automatically or quickly drawn to faith or church or even our community groups. Introducing people to Jesus for the first time can be awkward and clunky, but it makes sense to introduce people to Jesus in their natural habitat, where they can meet Him in real life, where He does His best work.

- Reflect on some of your relationships with non-Christians. What are some barriers between you and them that you could remove without compromising your faith?

- What are some things you can do so that you can connect with people around you who don't yet know Christ?

Adapted from *Interrupted*, copyright © 2014 by Jen Hatmaker. Used by permission of NavPress. All rights reserved. Represented by Tyndale House Publishers, Inc.

TRAIT FIVE:

Reproducing Spiritual Generations

Spiritual Generations

ARMANDO DIAZ

You then, my son, be strong in the grace
that is in Christ Jesus. And the things you
have heard me say in the presence of many
witnesses entrust to reliable people who
will also be qualified to teach others.

2 TIMOTHY 2:1-2

I MET HIM IN MIAMI. He was a young Christian with many questions. Even though everything seemed to be okay, he knew there was something missing: someone to lead him to a deeper relationship with God. As we talked we realized that God had brought him to our home to be discipled and trained—life on life, in the context of other young believers, and in a way that he could receive individual attention.

The next week we had our first one-on-one discipleship encounter; those encounters continued for two years. Later he enrolled in seminary, and now he serves God at his church as minister for outreach and small cell groups. His passion is to teach the same principles he has learned from me through the discipleship process; he prays to leave a legacy in other followers of Christ, who will help still more.

As the coming of Christ nears, it is imperative for us to obey what Paul told his disciple Timothy: "You then, my son, be strong in the grace that is in Christ Jesus. And the things you have heard me say in the presence of many witnesses entrust to reliable people who will also be qualified to teach others" (2 Timothy 2:1-2). What Paul told young Timothy applies for us today: We have received abundant grace through Christ, and God is calling us to teach this grace to reliable people, qualifying them to go on to teach others. God needs spiritual parents who spend time discipling the next generation of His people who will make Christ known among the nations. Are you willing to make your contribution?

- Reflect on people who have entrusted the teachings of Christ to you. Why did they invest in *you*?

- Whom in your life can you entrust with the teachings of Christ's grace and a relationship with Him? How will you work in such a way that they are equipped to help others also?

A Seed in the Right Soil

D. G. ELMORE

*Still other seed fell on good soil. It
came up and yielded a crop, a hundred
times more than was sown.*

LUKE 8:8

A FRIEND OF MINE likes to ask the question, "How
many seeds are in an apple?"

Now, neither my friend nor I have ever counted
the seeds in an apple. We like to follow up his question with a more interesting one: "How many apples
are in a seed?"

Jesus' parable in Luke 8 teaches us that investing
in the life of another person—planting the "seed" of
the Word of God and nurturing its growth—does not
always produce fruit. But when the "soil" is right—
when that person hears the Word we bring them,
retains it, and perseveres in it—the fruit of our investment will multiply for years to come.

As we look back at our own personal spiritual jour-
neys, we can recall those who have nurtured us in our
faith. We realize that we are part of a crop that extends
far beyond their initial investment. Our friends and
family whom we are helping come to know and love

Jesus are part of our crop; they are also the fruit of those who nurtured us.

God allows us to be part of future generations—to create a legacy. As my friends come to faith in Jesus and walk with Jesus through life, they in turn pass this on to their families and friends, who then lead changed lives and become yet another seed. The kingdom of God expands exponentially.

How many apples are in a seed? When planted in the right soil, an entire apple orchard.

- Thank God for the people who nurtured you in your faith. You are the fruit of their labors.

- Who are one or two people you are helping along in their relationships with Christ? Pray for them: They are your future generations—your legacy.

The Disciple Maker's
Central Message

MIKE JORDAHL

*For what we preach is not ourselves, but Jesus Christ
as Lord, and ourselves as your servants for Jesus' sake.*
2 CORINTHIANS 4:5

A FRIEND OF MINE once told me, "Mike, remember
that old news for you is headlines for them." Every
young believer who wants to become strong in his or
her faith and grow as a solid Christ-follower needs the
same things we needed as young believers: practical
help in developing spiritual habits that include prayer
and abiding in God's Word; a community of other
believers; an understanding of basic doctrine; reliance
on the Holy Spirit; and encouragement in sharing the
faith with others.

Sometimes, however, our equipping of others can
drift from these simple tools and the central message
of Jesus to something else: a certain doctrine, a favor-
ite author, a special ministry focus, or even a Bible
study method or spiritual discipline. Although they
certainly have some value, these should never become
the focus of our teaching and training of others.

At a time when I was on the hunt for the "latest

63

and greatest" in the realm of making disciples, my friend's words helped me adjust my focus. Disciple makers equip others to become firmly established as followers of Christ. Doing this well requires every disciple maker to ensure that Jesus Christ—and nothing else—is our central message.

- Have you allowed one of your "favorites" to become the center of your disciple making?

- How can you ensure that your central message is Jesus Christ and nothing else?

Spiritual Parenting

JIM AND BETH LUEBE

*For though you have countless guides in Christ,
you do not have many fathers. For I became your
father in Christ Jesus through the gospel.*
I CORINTHIANS 4:15, ESV

COUNTLESS PEOPLE are willing to come into and out of a person's life on a short-term basis. These may include wonderful speakers, teachers, and leaders. The apostle Paul sees such people as "guides." While guides serve important functions, their influence is appropriately limited. Guides may be many and valuable, and they may even be able to say they touched more people, but they don't compare to a spiritual parent.

The difference between being a guide and a spiritual parent is at the heart of what it means to "disciple" someone—that is, to help them grow as a follower of Christ. While a guide is present for a short time and in many cases is some distance removed, a parent is intimately involved in the lives of their sons or daughters. While a parent may not have the capacity to have as many "children" as a guide, a good parent is engaged, consistent, and faithful over time. Their love is sacrificial and unconditional.

The nature of spiritual parenting goes beyond sharing the truths of God's Word. Spiritual parents invest deeply, consistently, relationally, and with love in the people they are helping to follow Christ. It's this kind of relationship, this spiritual parenting, that is at the heart of disciple making.

- Reflect on the most significant spiritual influences in your life. What distinguishes the "guides" from the "parents"?

- How does this concept of "spiritual parenting" impact how you will help others become disciples of Jesus?

- Who around you needs the help of a "spiritual parent" and would be open to your influence?

The Influence in
Opening Our Lives

T. J. ADDINGTON

Because we loved you so much, we were delighted to share with you not only the gospel of God but our lives as well.
1 THESSALONIANS 2:8

THE MOST POWERFUL INFLUENCE is that of life on life, where who *we* are rubs off on others, influencing who *they* become. The guiding factor in that transaction is the ability of the others to know and understand us.

Opening our lives to others is much like opening our homes. It is an invitation to come in, make themselves comfortable, and commune as friends do. I may think I know someone well, but actually being in his or her home changes the equation because I see family interactions, the contents of bookshelves, and all kinds of interesting things.

The same is true with our lives. Opening our lives to others lets them into the genuine inner person. When we do so, whatever God is doing in the transformation of our lives becomes a point of connection in the lives of others—for us and for God, and therefore for influence.

We often read Paul's letters in a theological manner. And with reason, as Paul was the consummate theologian of the New Testament. But try reading them as letters of self-disclosure, in which Paul intentionally and openly shared his life, emotions, dreams, struggles, and even failures, and you see a person like you and me: straining to live out the call of God, becoming a man of God, and embracing the power of God.

As Jesus has called us to the same ministry that He performed (see John 17:18), it follows naturally that we should make the same effort to live transparently with others and make our lives accessible to them. Then we, like Jesus, have an amazing opportunity to influence others for Christ. He disclosed God to us through His life. We disclose Jesus to others through our lives.

- Read a passage from one of Paul's letters (for example, 2 Timothy). Write down what you observe about his life, emotions, dreams, struggles, and even failures.

- Who in your life would be helped in their faith by greater transparency from you?

Adapted from *Deep Influence*, copyright © 2014 by T. J. Addington. Used by permission of NavPress. All rights reserved. Represented by Tyndale House Publishers, Inc.

A Vision for the
Next Generation

OSAZE MURRAY

*Then David gave his son Solomon . . . the plans
of all that the Spirit had put in his mind.*
1 CHRONICLES 28:11-12

WHEN IT COMES to doing all that I want to do for
the Lord—even just accomplishing everything on my
to-do list as a husband, a dad, or a friend—I have my
limits.

I am not alone. We all are limited, and for many
different reasons. Some of our limitations are physical,
some are the result of past decisions, and we all face
certain limits we can only explain as God's sovereign
will. Looking at it more broadly, all of us are limited
to our time on earth. It doesn't matter how much
we desire to do for God and with God. We have to
embrace our limits.

Take David, for example. For many years his great
desire was to build "a house" for God—a Temple
where future generations could praise Yahweh. It was
not a part of God's plans, however, for the Temple
to be built in David's generation; instead David was
given the opportunity to pass along his vision to

Solomon. "Be strong," David told Solomon, "and do the work" (1 Chronicles 28:10).

David accepted the limits God set for his place in history, and the Temple was built with splendor and grandeur by the next generation—and enjoyed by many generations thereafter. It's this kind of humility in ministry that God uses to build His kingdom and bless all generations.

I might want to do great things for God, but it will likely not happen if I insist on it all happening through me. God's plans are bigger. He wants those around me and the next generation, too, to "catch the vision" of knowing Him and being used by Him. God wants us to pass along the message of His gospel and the know-how of following Him to the next generation—and to the generations after that!

- What limits have you been reluctant to embrace? How might embracing those limits serve a larger purpose in God's work in the world?

- Who around you may be God's way of extending your influence and His work to the next generation and beyond?

- How can you help those around you to "catch the vision" of following God?

Conclusion

WELL, IF YOU HAVE MADE IT to this point, I'm confident that your heart, thoughts, attitudes, and motivations for being used by God have been molded and clarified in the process.

Remember the sling-and-stone metaphor. The sling is the character of your life—the work of God in you that is the foundation for living out the five traits we've focused on in these pages. It's the character-transforming work of the Spirit in your soul—your identity in Christ; the fruit of the Spirit; the humble, servant attitude of Christ—that is the source of everything you lay your hand to.

The lifestyle that flows from these five traits—walking with Jesus, knowing and living the Scriptures, participating in community, engaging with those who don't know Christ, and reproducing spiritual generations of disciples of Jesus—is what we are destined for. This calling is meant for every season of life—during the ups and the downs, when we are amidst life transitions, and when life is more settled. We never are finished growing, so as disciples, we learn and grow, becoming more useful with each passing year as we embody the spirit of Jesus and communicate the message of the kingdom in each season.

I encourage you to take these ideas and blend them into the life, career, sphere of influence, and geography where Jesus has placed you. If you are just getting started, don't wait any longer! Life connected to the Lord Jesus is filled with joy, life-expanding trials, and heart-thumping thrills. A transforming relationship with God and partnership in His kingdom work is what Jesus offered His disciples over two thousand years ago: "Come with me. . . . I'll show you how to catch men and women instead of perch and bass" (Matthew 4:19, MSG).

Dr. Doug Nuenke

Contributors

Jerry Bridges is a speaker and the author of more than a dozen books, including *The Pursuit of Holiness*. Before joining Navigator staff, Jerry earned a degree in engineering and served as an officer in the Navy during the Korean Conflict.

Dr. Doug Nuenke serves as The Navigators' US president. He is passionate about helping his friends to know Jesus and to help others know Him. He enjoys developing leaders who reflect the Lord Jesus, and he loves to fish—for people and for trout!

Walking with Jesus

Joe Brown is an active-duty US Air Force officer currently stationed in Montgomery, Alabama. Joe is passionate about making disciples of Jesus and developing military leaders who, with Christlike character, see their profession as a sacred calling of kingdom work.

Martha Lawry works overseas as a personal assistant to the president of a private university. She lives with a local family there, loves languages, and is learning to play a local folk instrument.

John Starke has worked at The Advisory Board Company and now leads a ministry to men and women in their twenties in Atlanta. He is passionate about equipping the next generation of professionals to have effective ministry in their workplaces and communities.

Mark Kimmel spent many years walking with God while in corporate America, including in leadership positions in Harsco Corporation, New World Pasta Company, the Hershey Company, and The Navigators.

Gary L. Thomas is a teaching pastor at Second Baptist Church Houston. He has published sixteen books, including *Sacred Marriage* and *The Glorious Pursuit*.

Katie Hubbard loves training men and women on college campuses to live lives that are centered on Christ and overflowing with grace into the lives of others. She is a wife and a mother of four, and she enjoys having people in her home.

Knowing and Living the Scriptures

Lindy Black serves as associate US director of The Navigators, and she oversees staff care and development. She and her husband, Vic, have a passion for developing men and women to be all God designed them to be.

Steve Rugg was led to Christ through a friend in college, where he learned how to walk with Jesus and help others do the same. Steve currently leads a ministry initiative aimed to more effectively disciple people of all ethnic backgrounds.

Tom Yeakley has been coaching and developing leaders for more than thirty years. He has authored several books, is an international speaker, and is currently a field director for The Navigators.

Patriece Johnson and her husband, Dexter, minister among the US Air Force at Joint Base Charleston in South Carolina. Patriece is passionate about empowering and equipping women to be mature disciples of Jesus who in turn make disciples and labor for a lifetime.

Leonard Sweet is a theologian, semiotician, church historian, pastor, and author. He was a pioneer in advocating for the contextualization of Christianity into digital culture.

Joe Maschhoff lives with his family in the Dominican Republic as the Caribbean director for The Navigators. Joe has held multiple leadership roles in collegiate and young adult ministry and is passionate about calling people to greatness.

Participating in Community

Robert Daniels serves as the connections minister at The Village Church in Dallas, Texas, and is working toward a master's degree in theology at Dallas Theological Seminary. Robert and his wife, Whitney, hope to do inner-city ministry, planting churches that plant churches.

Brian Zaas and his wife, Debi, lead a growing team of more than sixty certified coaches as national directors for life and leadership coaching with The Navigators National Church Ministries. Their goal is to help churches become intentional disciple-making churches.

Felix Colonnieves served in the United States Air Force for twenty years as a helicopter pilot. He currently leads a military ministry to Air Force servicemen and servicewomen. He is passionate about advancing the gospel of Jesus and His kingdom on every Air Force base.

Jean Fleming is an author and speaker. She has lived and ministered all over the country and internationally with The Navigators for over fifty years. Jean is experienced in and passionate about helping women one-on-one to be disciples of Jesus.

Rachel Jones lives in east Africa with her husband and three children. She has written for *Christianity Today*, DesiringGod.org, and Her.meneutics.

Matt Letourneau is city director for The Navigators in Atlanta, overseeing numerous ministry initiatives. He is passionate about seeing the gospel reach into every ethnic and socioeconomic demographic of the city, and he loves sharing the gospel with those yet to follow Jesus.

Engaging with Those Who Don't Know Christ

Alan Andrews and his wife, Becky, live among and minister to an under-resourced community in Phoenix. They are living out their passion to help the poor know Jesus. Alan is a former US president of The Navigators.

Darrell and Cindy Jolley live in Dallas and minister to refugees from Africa, the Middle East, and Asia. Darrell works as a chief financial officer and Cindy is a former schoolteacher.

Jane Kirkpatrick is an author and internationally recognized speaker with more than one million copies of her books in print. Before beginning her career as an author, Jane was the first female president of the Oregon Community Mental Health Director's Association.

Al Engler met his wife, Iris, in Germany on a military assignment. They both met Jesus Christ on his second assignment to the country. They were trained in discipleship by The Navigators, and Al has since held many leadership positions in both the military and other ministry contexts.

Abu Mannar worked as a businessman in Singapore and now lives and works in Dallas. He and his wife, Suzy, teach others how to minister cross-culturally and are passionate about advancing the gospel in the lives of those of other faiths.

Jen Hatmaker is an author, blogger, television personality, and motivational speaker. Jen focuses on important topics such as American excess, family life, and wrecking comfortable Christianity.

Reproducing Spiritual Generations

Armando Diaz is a registered nurse and a gifted teacher and disciple. These diverse roles give him unique opportunities to be among the Hispanic community in Miami, sharing the Good News and discipling people. He is also associate director for The Navigators' Hispanic network.

D. G. Elmore is founder and owner of The Elmore Companies, companies that span multiple industries. D. G. also invests his time in discipling other businessmen and serving as chairman of The Navigators' board of directors.

Mike Jordahl is passionate about empowering men and women to live intentional and "missional" lives that are rooted in a vibrant relationship with God. He has held many leadership roles in ministry and currently serves as a field director for The Navigators.

Jim and Beth Luebe have been involved in discipling students for the last three decades, sending them to the nations both in-country and throughout the world. They serve as national leaders of The Navigators Collegiate Mission.

T. J. Addington is a senior vice president with the Evangelical Free Church of America (EFCA) and the leader of ReachGlobal, the international mission of the EFCA. He has served as a pastor and consultant and has authored several books.

Osaze Murray is a missionary to African American college students at Bowie State University, a historically black university. He is also a gospel rap artist, having recorded under the name Oppose. He loves sharing truths of God's Word through music.